WE CREATE

An Intro to the Principled Entrepreneur

Grady Connolly

Illustrated by Joanie McMahon

LUMINARE PRESS

WWW.LUMINAREPRESS.COM

Printed in the United States of America

Written by: Grady Connolly
Illustrated by: Joanie McMahon
Book Design by Claire Flint Last

Luminare Press
442 Charnelton St.
Eugene, OR 97401
www.luminarepress.com

LCCN: 2022906939
ISBN: 978-1-64388-900-9

For Mom & Dad.
Your love, faith, and charity provide me
with an example to follow.

Mom, can you tell me about your work?

Well, I work as a Principled Entrepreneur.

Entrepreneurs are people
who start businesses.

Principled Entrepreneurs try to
do the right thing and start businesses
that make life better for others.

We create your favorite gadgets and gizmos.

We explore new ideas,

embracing our creative spirit.

We dream big

despite the world's advice to think small and seek safety.

We create jobs

so everyone can discover their unique talents
through meaningful work.

We solve problems,

making life better
for others.

We take risks

because bravery makes us stronger.

We are honest,

keeping promises to
earn the trust of others.

We ask questions

and have the courage
to challenge how things
have always been done

We put people first

because every human being is important.

We build communities,

celebrating everyone's unique contribution.

We take time for self-care,

maintaining health of mind, body and soul.

We help other creators,

providing support throughout their journey.

We look forward
to the future

and find joy and gratitude in the present.

Mom, why did YOU become a
Principled Entrepreneur?

There are many reasons.

People who do the work I do want to make
a difference in the lives of others.

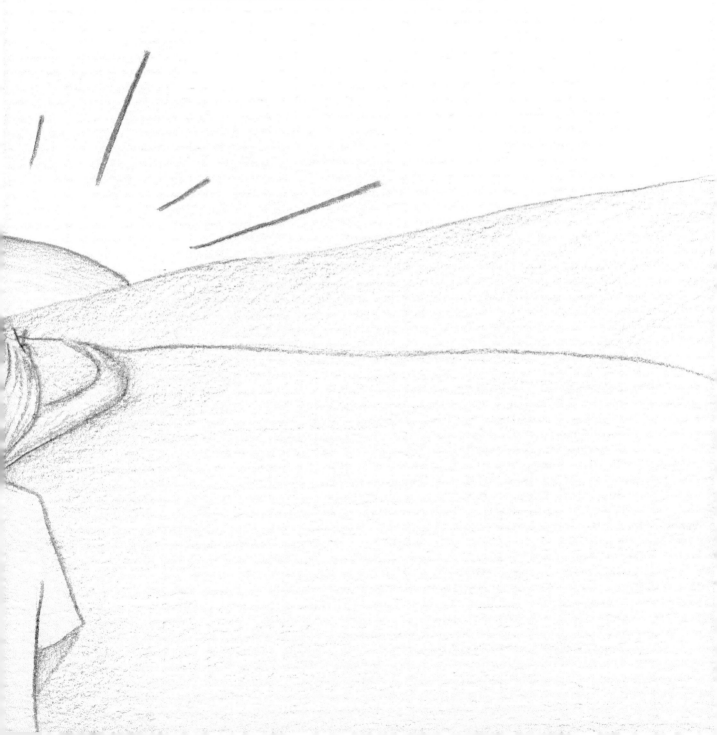

We love to give back
and help others,

making the world a better place through our
success, wisdom, wealth, and ideas.

We share our time

to give others the opportunity to
learn from our experiences.

We donate to schools

to help children learn.

We donate to hospitals

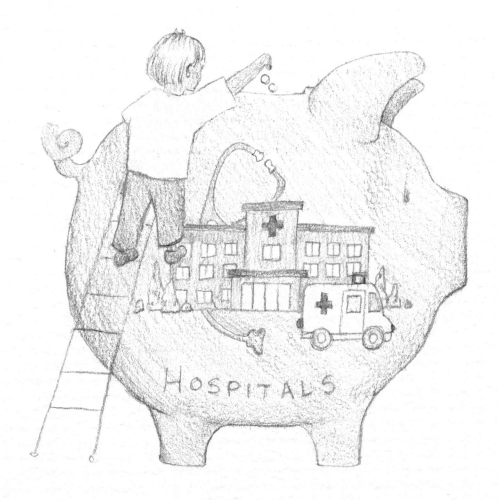

so that we may all live long, healthy lives.

We donate to houses of worship

so that everyone has a place to reflect and pray.

We fight for equal rights

to ensure everyone has the chance to flourish.

We believe in the power of dreams

and the ability for yours to come true
through hard work and dedication.

Being a Principled Entrepreneur
is not always easy.

It requires a lot of work.

It is risky.

There is a lot of responsibility.

Making an impact makes it worthwhile.

The fruits of what we create are long lasting
and will be enjoyed by all.

So keep your eyes open, your mind alert,
and your creative spirit awake

and you can be a Principled Entrepreneur too.

Special thanks to

Andreas Widmer, Luke Burgis, and Brian Walsh
for introducing me to the art of Principled Entrepreneurship.
Their virtuous leadership is something we can all learn from.
Be sure to check out their books, businesses, and projects.

Did you love this book?

Please consider writing a review on Amazon, spreading
the word on social media, and/or grabbing a copy for a friend.
Your generous support helps spread this message far and wide.

Thank you.

About the Author

GRADY CONNOLLY is a creator who believes that business can be a powerful force for good. He received his Bachelor's Degree in Business from The Catholic University of America where he studied alongside renowned entrepreneurs at The Ciocca Center for Principled Entrepreneurship. Grady has worked with startup companies across consumer technology, social media, non-profit, and entertainment. Outside his work in the startup ecosystem, he enjoys attending concerts and shows, traveling, and searching for the most beautiful works of sacred art, music, and architecture during his adventures.

@thegradyconnolly

About the Illustrator

JOANIE MCMAHON is an artist based out of upstate New York with a Bachelor of Arts in Studio Art from The Catholic University of America. She works primarily in portraiture but also enjoys creating whimsical illustrations of everyday life. She believes in uplifting the beauty of the ordinary and can often be found painting the squirrels that terrorize her backyard.

@mcmahonart_

A special thank you to our sponsors
TIM AND STEPH BUSCH

Born in Michigan, Tim relocated to sunny Southern California where he met his wife, Steph. Married for 36 years, they have two children and eight grandchildren.

Tim is principal shareholder of Busch Firm, an Irvine law firm established in 1979 which specializes in estate planning, asset protection, tax, real estate, and corporate law litigation, in addition to representing religious organizations. He has various affiliations in private operating and real estate companies, including Pacific Hospitality Group, which owns and operates thirteen hotels, such as Meritage Collection Brand hotels in Napa and Huntington Beach, California, Austin, Texas, and Kauai, Hawaii. Tim also owns Busch's Markets, which operates sixteen high-end grocery stores in southeastern Michigan.

Since 1990, Tim and Steph have been active members of Legatus, an organization for Catholic CEOs and their spouses.

Long time advocates of private Catholic schooling, Tim and Steph cofounded St. Anne School in Laguna Niguel in 1992, a private Roman Catholic school with enrollment of 650 students. Steph served as COO for fourteen years and is now on the Executive Committee at the grade school where both their children graduated and six of their grandchildren attend. Tim and Steph also cofounded JSerra Catholic High School, a private

Roman Catholic School in San Juan Capistrano that has an enrollment of over 1,300. The Catholic University of America, a Pontifical University in Washington, DC, named its business school the Tim and Steph Busch School of Business. Tim serves as chair of the school's Board of Visitors and is on the Board of Visitors of the Institute for Human Ecology.

Tim and Steph cofounded the Magis Institute with Fr. Robert Spitzer, SJ. The Magis Institute runs the Reason and Faith Center and the Napa Institute.

Tim and Steph both serve on Board of The Institute for Church Life at the University of Notre Dame. Steph also serves on the boards of Obria Orange County and St. Anne School, while Tim serves as chair of the Magis Institute, the Napa Institute, and the Napa Legal Institute, in addition to serving on the board of EWTN.

Tim and Steph enjoy traveling, wine, and golfing. They reside in Laguna Hills, California and maintain vacation residences in New York, and Napa and Indian Wells, California.